HBJ BOOKMARK READING PROGRAM

Margaret Early

Elizabeth K. Cooper

Nancy Santeusanio

Together We Go

Stories and articles by

Elizabeth K. Cooper

HARCOURT BRACE JOVANOVICH

New York *Chicago* *San Francisco* *Atlanta* *Dallas* **and** *London*

Contents

Requests for permission to make copies of any part of the work should be mailed to: Permissions; Harcourt Brace Jovanovich, Inc.; 757 Third Avenue; New York, New York 10017.

Printed in the United States of America   ISBN 0–15–331781–7

ACKNOWLEDGMENTS: For permission to reprint copyrighted material, grateful acknowledgment is made to the following sources:

Harcourt Brace Jovanovich, Inc.: "For a Bird" from *The Moon and a Star* by Myra Cohn Livingston. Copyrighted © 1965 by Myra Cohn Livingston.
Harper & Row, Publishers, Inc.: "Robert, Who Is Often a Stranger to Himself" from *Bronzeville Boys and Girls* by Gwendolyn Brooks. Copyrighted © 1956 by Gwendolyn Brooks Blakely.
Katherine Edelman Lyon, Literary Executrix for Katherine Edelman: "September Morning" by Katherine Edelman. Reprinted from *Child Life* Magazine, 1956.
Parents' Magazine Press: "The House That Nobody Wanted" from *Junk Day On Juniper Street* by Lilian Moore. Copyrighted © 1968 by Lilian Moore.

School Days

$$\begin{array}{r} 6 \\ +\ 3 \\ \hline 9 \end{array}$$

QqRr

Going to School

In the morning, boys and girls get up.

They go to school.

Pam's house is just down the street from the school.

In the morning, Pam goes to the street.

She stops and looks.

Then she crosses the street.

She gets her friend, Jill.

The friends run to school.

The school is far away from
Tim's house.

Tim rides to school in a bus.

In the morning, he waits by
his house.

The big school bus comes down
the hill and stops.

Tim gets on the bus.

He rides to school with his friends.

Stan's house is in a big city.

In the morning, Stan rides to school in a train.

The train goes up the city streets. Stan gets a fast ride to school.

Some boys and girls ride to school
in cars.

Kim and Ted do that.
They ride with Father.
Up and down hills they go.
They ride past beautiful big rocks.
They see a rabbit by the rocks.
Kim and Ted like the ride to
school a lot.

Linda goes to school in a boat!

Water is all around Linda's house.

In the morning, Linda gets into the boat with Mother.

The boat crosses the water to the land.

Linda gets up from the boat.

Then she runs to school.

Fay's house is far away from
her school.

When Fay goes to school, she is
away for many days.

Fay's friend, Mr. Gray, comes to
her house.

He lands in the pond by her house.

Fay says good-by to her mother
and father.

Then she gets in.

Fay rides up into the sky.

Fay rides to school.

Boys and girls come up the street.
They come by car.
They come by train.
They come by bus.
Some run, and some ride.
They all come to school.

What did you do to get to school
this morning?

(To be read by the teacher.)

Morning

School is waiting,
Can't be late!
Hurry, hurry!
Half-past eight!
Out the door
And down the street
Then softly, quietly
Take your seat.

KATHERINE EDELMAN

13

No, it wasn't so bad.
We had to run to school.
It is fun to run in the rain.

It was good, then.

No, it wasn't very good at all.
We got to the top of a hill.
A big truck went by and splashed me.

That was bad!

Ben's Surprise

Ben was going up the street with a box.

He was going to school.

Ben saw his friend, Stan.

Stan ran up and said, "Show me what you have in the box, Ben."

"No," said Ben.

"It is a surprise.

It is my pet."

The boys went up the street.
Kim looked out and saw them.
"Wait for me!" she called.

Kim ran out to her friends.
"What is in the box?" asked Kim.

"Ben will not tell," said Stan.

"Well, I'll tell you this," said Ben.
"My pet is little and green."

When the children were at the school they saw Mr. Park.

"Is that your lunch box, Ben?" asked Mr. Park.

"That is Ben's surprise," said Kim.

"It is a little green pet," said Stan.

"Yes, and it lives by a pond," said Ben.

Mr. Park said, "Well, I do not know what it is.

I'll go in with you and find out."

In the school they saw the
teacher, Mrs. Wolf.

"Good morning," she said.

"What is that, Ben?"

"That is Ben's surprise," said
Mr. Park.

"It is a little green pet," said Kim.

"It lives by a pond," said Stan.

"It hops, too," said Ben.

"A little green pet that lives by
a pond and hops?" said Mrs. Wolf.

"What is it?"

"Yes, show us!" said Mr. Park.

"Please!" said Kim and Stan.

Ben laughed and said, "Look!"
They all looked.

"Oh," they said, "**that** is what it is."

Do you know what Ben's surprise was?

Frogs

If you are looking for a frog, go to a pond.

That is where frogs live.

Frogs never live very far from a pond, for a frog needs water.

But a frog cannot live under the water.

A frog needs air, too.

25

Frogs come from tadpoles.
Where do tadpoles come from?
Tadpoles come out of frog eggs.
The eggs are in pond water.
Tadpoles are not at all like frogs.
Tadpoles can live under the water.
They do not need to come up
for air.

Tadpoles do not look like frogs.
Frogs have big legs in back.
They have little legs in front.
But tadpoles have no legs.
They cannot run and jump.

What can a tadpole do?
A tadpole lives under the water.
It eats green things that grow in
the pond.
It gets big.

Soon the tadpole grows legs in back.

It grows legs in front, too.

At last the day comes when the tadpole can live on land.
It comes out of the water.
It hops on the grass.
It sits by the pond.
It is a little frog.

28

The little frog lives on the land.
It finds bugs and things to eat.
It eats and eats.

One day it is not a little frog.
It is a big green frog that lives
by the pond.

Chuggarum!

I once saw a big green frog,
   Chuggarum
A great big bass-drum frog,
   Chuggarum
It sat on a log
In a dark wet bog
And it waited for flies to come,
   Chuggarum!

I'd much rather go to school,
   Chuggarum
Than sit by a splashy pool,
   Chuggarum
And hope that a fly
Will wander by —
I'd rather chew bubble gum.
   Chuggarum!

Animal Fun

The Little Red Hen

This is a play for you to do.
You will need children to play

The Little Red Hen
The Duck
The Mouse
The Rabbit

RED HEN: I have four bags of
wheat seeds.
I will plant the seeds on the hill.
But I need help.
Who will help me plant the wheat?

DUCK: Not I! I am playing.

MOUSE: Not I! I am looking for rocks.

RABBIT: Not I! I must go to sleep.

RED HEN: Then I'll plant the wheat myself.

BOYS: And she did.

A GIRL: Little Red Hen planted the
wheat on the hill.
By the end of summer, the
wheat was up.

RED HEN: It is time to cut the wheat.
But I need help.
Who will help me cut the wheat?

DUCK: Not I! I must go to the city.

MOUSE: Not I! I cannot work in
the sun.

RABBIT: Not I! I am not well today.

RED HEN: Then I'll cut the wheat myself.

GIRLS: And she did.

A BOY: Little Red Hen cut the wheat.
She put the wheat in bags.
She had four bags of wheat.

RED HEN: I will make this wheat
into flour.
But I need help.
Who will help me make the flour?

DUCK: Not I! I must look for my hat.

MOUSE: Not I! I must go to the park.

RABBIT: Not I! I cannot make flour.

RED HEN: Then I'll make the flour myself.

BOYS: And she did.

A GIRL: Little Red Hen worked to
make the wheat into flour.

RED HEN: I have four bags of flour.
I will bake a cake.
But I need help.
Who will help me bake a cake?

DUCK: Not I! I must get some water.

MOUSE: Not I! I am going to a party.

RABBIT: Not I! I cannot bake a cake.

RED HEN: Then I'll bake the cake myself.

GIRLS: And she did.

39

A BOY: Little Red Hen had a cake.
It was the best cake of all time.
Then she sent for her friends.

RED HEN: I have this cake.
Who will help me eat it?

DUCK, MOUSE, RABBIT: I will!

RED HEN: No, you will not!
I planted the wheat myself.
I cut the wheat myself.
I got the flour myself.
And I had to bake this
cake myself.
You did not help me make it.
So you will not help me eat it.
I will eat all the cake myself!

ALL: And she did!

Making a Set

It is fun to put on a play.

You can put on "The Little Red Hen" at school.

But first, make a set for it.

Making the set is fun, too.

The set is a big picture.

It is a house and plants.

It shows where the animals in the play lived.

Make a big picture.

Paint the land of the Little Red Hen.

Paint the hill where she planted
the wheat.

Paint a blue sky.

Paint some green grass.

Paint some red and blue flowers
growing in the grass.

You can make a house for the
Little Red Hen.

Get a big box.

Cut out one side of the box.

Work on the inside of the box.

Make it look like the Little Red
Hen's house.

Paint the outside, too.

Then make some wheat plants.
Paint the wheat plants.
Cut them out.
Put them on a chair, as you see here.
You have made a good set.
You can put on the Little Red Hen
play for your friends.

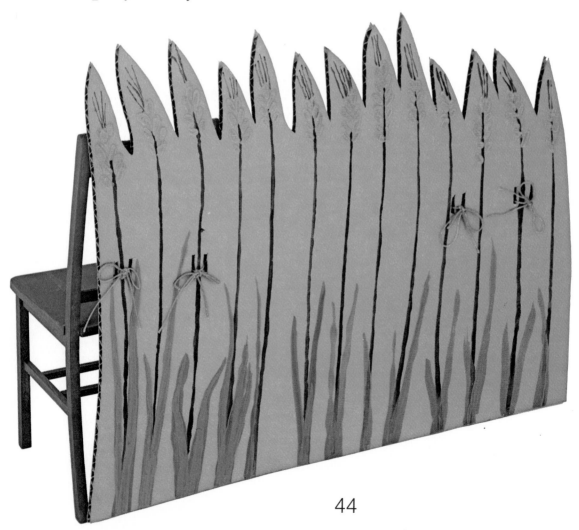

The Clay House

The Lost Jar

One day a woman was going to
the city.

She had bright blue jars in
her wagon.

But she lost one jar in the grass.
She did not see the jar go down.
So the woman did not stop.
She went on over the hill.

45

A little mouse ran up to the jar.
He said, "This looks like a good
clay house.
I'll see who lives in it.
Who is in this clay jar?"

All was still.
The mouse climbed into the jar.
"It is not cracked," he said.
"It is clean inside.
It will make a good house for me."

Soon a little duck came flying
over the grass.

She went up to the clay jar.

"This looks like a clay house,"
she said.

"I'll see who is in it.

Who is in this clay house?"

"I am," cried the mouse.
"Who are you?"

"I am a little duck," said
the duck.
"Can I please come in?"

"Yes, yes.
Come in," said the mouse.

The duck climbed in and
looked around.
"I am glad I came here,"
said the duck.

Soon a little hen came down the hill.
She went up to the clay jar.
"This is a clay house," she said.
"I will see who is in it.
Who is in this clay house?"

"We are," cried the mouse and duck.
"But who are you?"

"I am a little hen.
Can I please come into your
house?" asked the hen.

"Yes, yes.
Come in," said the duck.

The hen climbed in and looked
around the jar.
"I am glad I came," she said.

The Great Big Bear

That afternoon, a great big bear
came down from the hills.
He went over to the jar.
"What a funny clay house," he said.
"I'll see who is in it."

50

The bear called, "Who is in this
little house?"

"We are," cried the mouse.
"But who are you?"

"I am a great big bear.
Can I come into your house?"

The animals looked at the bear.
"No, you cannot," said the hen.
"You are much too big for this
little house."

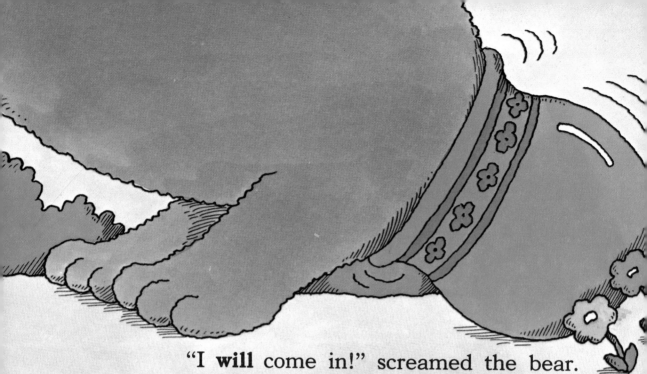

"I **will** come in!" screamed the bear.

"You are too big," said the duck.

The bear sat down.
He backed into the clay house.
"You will break the jar!" called
the mouse.

The bear backed in some more.
"Please stop!" screamed the animals.
"Do not break the clay house!"

But the bear did not stop.
He backed in some more.

"Run out the back door!"
called the mouse.

Crack went the clay house.

Crack!

CRACK!

Then the clay house was all
over the grass.

"Oh no," cried the bear.
"What did I do?"

"You silly bear," called the mouse.

"A great big bear cannot get into a little clay house.

You are too big!"

The mouse, duck, and hen went away.

But the bear just sat under the tree and cried.

The Big Race

A rabbit met a turtle.
"I will race you up that hill,"
said the rabbit.

"I cannot race," said the turtle.
"Look at my little legs."

The rabbit made fun of the turtle.
"You are scared," said the rabbit.

That made the turtle mad.
"I'll race you," he said.

At that, the rabbit's big ears went back.

He got down.

He got set for the race.

"Are you set, Turtle?" he asked.

"All set," said the turtle.

"Go!" cried the rabbit.

The rabbit raced away.

The turtle walked, but not very fast.

The big race was on.

It was a bright summer day,
and the sun was hot.

The rabbit raced up the hill.
Then he looked back.
He did not see the turtle.

"I can take my time at this,"
said the rabbit.

"That turtle will never get to
the top of the hill first.

I'll just sit under this tree."

The rabbit sat down.
Soon he went to sleep.

The turtle just walked on and on.
He went as fast as a turtle can go.
And that is not very fast.
But he did not stop.

At last the turtle came to the
rabbit under the tree.
The rabbit was sleeping.
The turtle did not wake the
rabbit up.
He just went on up the hill.

When the rabbit jumped up, the
sun was far down in the sky.

"That was a good sleep," he said.
"Now I'll get this race over with."

The rabbit raced up the hill.
And he had a surprise.
The turtle was waiting at the top!

"You are too late," said the turtle.
"You can run fast.
But you still lost the race.
In a race, you must not stop.
You must go on and on and on."

Over in the Flowers

Over in the flowers
In the bright hot sun
Lived a big mother turtle
And her little turtle one.
"Play," said the mother.
"I will play," said the one.
"I will play all day
In the bright hot sun."

60

Over in the flowers
Where the pond is blue
Lived a big father duck
And his little ducks two.
"Splash," said the father.
"We will splash," said the two.
"We will splash all day
Where the pond is blue."

Over in the flowers
By a dark green tree
Lived a big mother rabbit
And her little rabbits three.
"Hop," said the mother.
"We will hop," said the three.
"We will hop all day
By the dark green tree."

Over in the flowers
By a big red door
Lived a mother and a father
And the little children four.
"Dance," said the father.
"We will dance," said the four.
"We will dance all day
By the big red door."

What Now, Bear?

Bear is hungry.
He looks for lunch.

Bear is still hungry.
He needs some lunch.

The bees are mad!

Pull, Bear, pull!

What will go on?

63

Will Bear get wet?

Bear is very hungry.

So are the people.

Will Bear eat lunch?

Bear is so hungry!
Bear is so sad!

The people like Bear.

Will Bear get lunch?

New Things
from
Old

What Is It?

At first it was a tree.
Then the tree was cut down.
Now it is not a tree.
Can you name what it is?

You can see it in your school.
You can see it in your house.
It is good for many things.

Many things are made of it.
Party hats and games are
made of it.
Pictures are painted on it.

You can cut it.
You can put it around a box.
You can make lines on it.
You can see it in this book.
It is in all your books.
Can you name it?

The five things you see here are
made of paper.

Can you name them?

Are you surprised at some
of them?

Can you find things around
you that are made of paper?

Once people did not have paper.
They did not have many of the
things we have now.

Did they have paper to paint on?
Did they have paper bags
and boxes?
Did they have books to read?
No, they did not.
But now we have paper, and we
make it into many, many things.

69

Trees and Paper

Look at the picture.
The trees are made of wood.
Paper is made from wood, too.

70

People come with saws.
Soon the trees are cut down.
Then they are cut into logs.

New trees are planted.
One day, those trees will grow
big, and then they will be cut
down, too.

Ropes are put around the logs.
The logs are put on big trucks.
The trucks drive out of the woods.
They go to a mill.

At the mill, big saws cut up the logs.

The wood is put into very hot water.

Many things are put in with the wood until it gets very soft.

The soft wood goes to a paper mill.
It is made into paper.
From the paper mill, the paper
comes to us.

Paper Nests

Once people did not have paper.

After a time they made paper
out of grasses.

Today people make paper from wood.

Were people the first to make paper?
No.
Wasps made paper first.
Wasps made paper from wood!

Look at the picture.
It shows a wasp's nest.
The nest is made out of paper.

What does a wasp do to make paper?
First it finds a good spot for a nest.
Then it finds some wood.

It chews the wood.
It chews and chews until the
wood is soft.
The wasp builds a nest with
the soft wood.

It makes many small rooms.

The rooms are for the wasp's eggs.

When the nest is made, it looks like paper.

It is paper.

It is a paper nest made by a wasp.

A Picture Book

You can make many things from paper.

One good thing to make is a picture book.

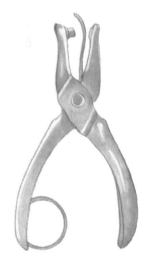

Get some sheets of paper.
Make the sheets into a book, like this.

A book has a name.

The name tells what the book is about.

Make up a name for your book.

Will you make a book about big city buildings?

About the sun and stars?

About animals at the zoo?

Will the book tell about cars?

What about a book on rain and snow?

A book about boats is fun.

So is a book about pets.

Make two lines on the first sheet
of your book.
 Put the name of your book on top.
 Then put your name under it.

Paint a picture on the next sheet in the book.

Make some lines under it.

On the lines, tell something about the picture.

Paint pictures on all the sheets.

Put something under all the pictures.

Then show the book to your friends.

Let them read the beautiful book that you have made.

Color Magic

A book with bright pictures is
fun to look at.
So is a circus with many colors.
Look at the picture of the circus.
Do you see bright red and yellow?
Do you see bright blue?

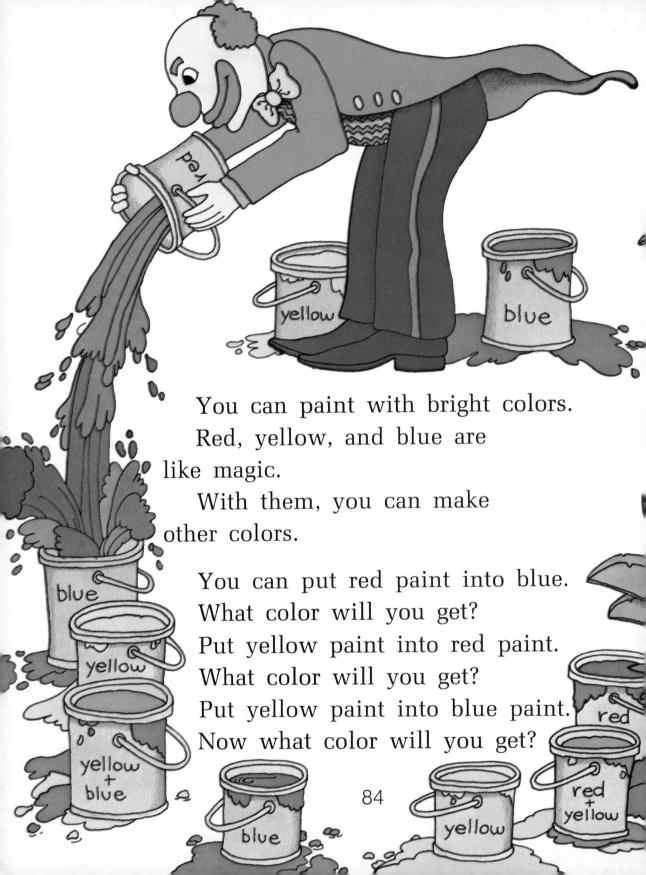

You can paint with bright colors.
Red, yellow, and blue are
like magic.
With them, you can make
other colors.

You can put red paint into blue.
What color will you get?
Put yellow paint into red paint.
What color will you get?
Put yellow paint into blue paint.
Now what color will you get?

84

Colors can be soft, too.

Look at this picture of some gentle woods.

Some of the colors are light. Other colors are dark.

What light green things do you see?

What dark green things do you see?

85

You can make light green paint.
Put a little yellow paint into some dark green paint.
You can make dark green, too.
Put a little blue paint into some light green paint.

Look around.
Colors are all around you.
Do you think colors are like magic?
What makes them like magic?

86

The Beautiful Turtle

Turtle was very good at singing.
His singing was so good that it made
all the animals in the woods dance.
They danced and laughed, oh yes.
"Sing, Turtle!" they called.
"We like to dance when you sing."

But was Turtle happy?

No, he was not.

He looked at his gentle friend, Bird, and said, "I do not want to sing.

I want to be beautiful, like you."

Bird said, "But your singing is very beautiful."

"No, no," said Turtle.

"I must get some bright feathers to put on my back.

Then I will be beautiful."

Bird laughed and said, "Here, take four of my feathers.

My friends will let you have some feathers, too."

"Thank you, Bird," said Turtle. "Then I will be beautiful."

Many of Bird's friends came with feathers.

Soon, Turtle had many feathers on his back.

The feathers were bright red and bright blue.

They were bright yellow and bright green.

All the bright colors were on Turtle's back.

That morning Turtle walked in the woods.

He looked very grand, oh yes!

All at once, Bird called out, "A man is in the woods.

Run fast and hide, Turtle."

Turtle ran to a tree.
"I'll hide here," he said.

"He will see your feathers," said Bird.

Turtle ran to a big rock.
"No, he will see you," called Bird.

Turtle cried, "What bad luck!
My feathers are too bright."

Soon the man saw Turtle.
He picked Turtle up.
"Oh, so many colors," said the man.
"But under the bright feathers I
see a turtle.
I'll have turtle soup for lunch."

Turtle cried, "This is the end of me.
I cannot get away, Bird."

"You can," called Bird.
"Sing, and make the man dance."

So Turtle did that.
What a surprise for the man!
He let go of Turtle and danced.
He danced around in the grass.
He danced out of the woods.
He danced over a hill.
He did not stop until he was far,
far away.

Bird said, "You do not need bright
feathers, Turtle.

You can sing."

"That is so," said Turtle.
"I will get rid of the feathers."
And he did.

"And I will sing!" said Turtle.
Then Turtle did that, oh yes.
All the animals danced and danced.
And Turtle was very happy, oh yes!

Bear Makes Some Paper

Plant trees.

Saw logs.

Go to the mill.

Cut down trees.

Make paper.

Water trees.

Help Bear make some paper.
The pictures show what Bear must do.
But they do not tell when to do it.
Take out some paper.
Put 1 on the top line.
What must Bear do first?
Put that next to the 1.
Put 2 on the next line.
Put down what Bear must do next.
Go on with lines 3, 4, 5, and 6.

Thank you!

95

A Paper Dog

Bear has lots of paper.
Now he is going to make something.
You can make it, too.
First, get some paper.

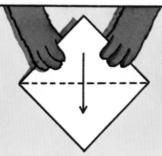

Fold down top of paper.

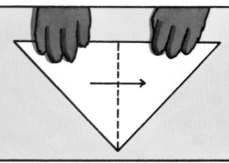

Fold over, then back.

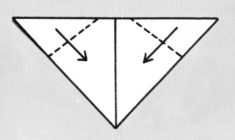

Fold down two ears.

Put in the eyes.

Look at what Bear has made!
Did you make a dog, too?

New Friends

Robert, Who is Often a Stranger to Himself

Do you ever look in the looking-glass
And see a stranger there?
A child you know and do not know,
Wearing the clothes you wear?

GWENDOLYN BROOKS

98

The New Boy in School

It was the first day in the new school for Luis Martinez.

He did not like it at all.

He did not like the school.

He did not like the new room.

The books were new to Luis.

So were all the children.

Luis did not do a thing.

He just sat and looked at his shoes.

Chet looked over at Luis.

Chet said to his friends, "On my first day here, I did that.

I sat and looked at my shoes.

I remember."

The children worked on their pictures, but Luis did not.

He did not do a thing all morning.

When the morning was over, the children had their lunches.

Luis sat by Mr. White, the teacher. He did not eat a thing.

Chet said to his friends, "I did not eat a thing on my first day. I remember."

After lunch, the boys and girls
went outside and played.

But Luis did not go out.
He just sat in the chair.
Then he cried.

Chet looked in the window at Luis.
Chet said, "When I was new here,
I cried, too.
I remember."

Chet went up to Mr. White.
Then he ran inside to Luis.

Luis said, "Who are you?"

Chet said, "My name is Chet.
I remember when I was new here.
I was scared, and I cried, just like you.
But I made some friends.
Now I like school.
Will you come out and play?"

Soon Chet and Luis came out.
They ran down the walk.
"Luis is happy now," said Chet.

"Come play over here," said Linda.

Chet said, "Luis will play with
you soon.
But today he is going to play
with me.
Luis is my friend first."

Betsy's Tomorrow

Betsy's things were all over her room.

She was in her room when her father came to the door.

"Betsy," he said.

"Get to work and put your things away."

Betsy looked around.
"What things, Dad?" she asked.

"What things?" said her father.
"I see books in front of the window.
Put away your old games.
Clean up the things on the chair.
Put away those paints."

"But Dad," said Betsy, "I have
lots of school work to do.
I can clean up my room tomorrow."

After school the next day, Betsy got to work.

She put away the old games.
Then she picked up a book.
She sat down to read the book.
It was called I Told You So.
It was a very funny book.

Betsy spent the afternoon reading.
"I'll clean up this room tomorrow," said Betsy.

The next day Betsy came in from school and got to work.

She put away some books.

Then she saw her pet mouse.

"I'll get you something to eat, Little Gray," said Betsy.

She did that.

Then Betsy spent the afternoon playing with Little Gray.

All at once, Betsy looked up.
Her father was standing at the door.
He looked mad.
"I told you to clean up this room,"
he said.

"But Dad, I had to look after
my mouse," Betsy said.
"I'll clean up the room tomorrow."

The next day was not a school day.
Betsy's father came to her room.
Betsy said, "I cannot clean the
room this morning, Dad.
I have to go to Jack's party.
All the children are going."

"I know one girl who is not going," said Betsy's father.

"That girl is staying here to clean up her room."

"No, Dad, no!" said Betsy.
"I'll do it first thing tomorrow."

"Not tomorrow, but now!" said Dad.
Betsy was not happy.
But she got to work.
Betsy's tomorrow had come!

Happy, Scared

I did it!
I did it!
I did it all by myself.
I climbed up the big tree.
And no one had to help me.

She was my friend.
Once we went to the park.
We skipped up the walk.
We saw a big red bug.
We had so much fun.
I wish she had not moved away.

They make me so mad.
They scold me.
They say I am too little.
I'll show them that I can do it, too.

I got on the fast ride.
I was so scared!
But it was so much fun.
I want to do it again.

She never says, "I have work to do."
She says, "Come and sit by me.
I'll read you a book."
I sit next to her.
And we read the book.

My Friend, Pete

Pete Gets Mad at Me

Pete is my best friend.
I walk to school with Pete.
I sit next to Pete at school.
After school, Pete and I play at his house.

But I will never forget the day that Pete got mad at me.
I did something very wrong.
And I lost my best friend.

We were walking to Pete's house
after school.

Pete said, "Come on in, Maria.
I'll show you my new pet."

I said, "Oh, boy, what is it?"

"You will see," said Pete.
We ran into the house and up to
Pete's room.

"Here it is," said Pete.

Pete's pet was a bird.

It was beautiful.

It was little, and it had green
and yellow feathers.

It was singing in the cage.

"Boy!" I said.

"Can I look at it?"

I got the cage down.

"Look out, Maria," said Pete.

"I will," I said.

But I did not look out.
I knocked over the cage!

"Oh, no!" said Pete.
His bird was out of the cage.
"Get it!" Pete cried.

We ran after the bird, but it
got away.
It went out the window and
over the trees.

Pete and I looked as his bird went over a big building.

Then Pete looked at me.

He said, "You let my bird get away."

"I am sorry," I said.

"You wanted to let it get away," said Pete.

"You did not want me to have a pet."

"You are wrong!" I said.

"You get out of here!" Pete called.
"Go on, get out!"

I ran out of Pete's house and down the street.

I went into the park and sat down.

My best friend was mad at me.

My best friend?

I knew that Pete was not my best friend.

Not now.

Doing Something About It

When I got home, Mother said,
"Is something wrong, Maria?"

"Oh, I had a bad day," I said.

I went up to my room and sat down.
I had to think.
Pete was my best friend, and I had
lost his pet bird.
I had to do something.
But what?

I looked at Mike, my pet.
Then I knew what I had to do.
I went over to Mike.

"You are my best pet," I said.
"But from now on you will not
be mine.
You will be Pete's pet.
You will help Pete forget about
the bird I lost."

I walked up the street with the cage.

I was very sad.

I did not want to let Pete have
my pet.

But I had to.

I came to Pete's house.

I knocked on the door and went in.

Pete saw me.

His eyes were red.

He said, "What do you want?
Get out of here!"

"Here," I said.
"This is for you."

Pete looked at Mike.
Then he looked at me.
He said, "You want me to have Mike?"

"Yes," I said.

Pete said, "Mike is your best pet."

"Yes, he is," I said.
"But he is not mine now."

I gave the cage to Pete.
He said, "Thanks, Maria, thanks a lot."
After that we were friends again.

We looked and looked for Pete's bird.
But we did not find it.
I am sorry about that.
Mike is Pete's pet now.
I am sorry about that, too.
But Pete is still my best friend.
And I am **not** sorry about that.

Bear at Work

Bear needs help fast! He must make some new words for the next story.

Put in 2 words. Out comes a new word.

Oh no, Bear! The word <u>day</u> cannot go with the word <u>after</u>. Can you help Bear make the new words?

after	hill	moon	thing
birth	side	moon	to
down	noon	out	man
grass	where	some	light
in	day	up	side
some	hopper	in	hill

127

Find 8 of Bear's new words in this story.

"What do you want to do on your birthday, Bear?" asked Turtle.

"I want to go somewhere," said Bear.

"I'll go to the moon."

Bear landed on the moon.

"I want to go outside and walk all around," he said.

He went out and looked around.

He ran uphill and downhill.

Then he saw something odd.

"Is that a moonman?" Bear cried.

"It looks like a grasshopper!"

Bear walked up to the moonman.

Then Turtle surprised him.

"Wake up, Bear," Turtle called.

"It is time to get up now."

128

The Worlds of Art

The Animal Art Show

Donkey, Sheep, Bear, and Fox
were good friends.
They met one day in the park.
Fox said, "Look at this, friends."

"Read it to us," said Sheep.

Fox said, "Art show tomorrow.
Make a work of art.
You can get a prize."

"We can all make something for the show," said Bear.

"Good thinking!" said Donkey.

"What can we make?" said Sheep.
"We are not very good at art."

"Make what you like," said Fox.
"We will all make things.
Then we will make a big work of art out of them."

"We have to be quick about it," said Donkey.
They ran home and got to work.

The next day the friends came back to the park.

Bear had what looked like a big green tree.

Donkey had flowers that he had made out of cans.

Sheep had a bright yellow sun.

And Fox had a big red star.

Bear put his tree on the grass.
Then Sheep gave Bear the sun,
star, and flowers.

"It looks great," said Bear.
"It will get a prize."

"No, it is all wrong," said Donkey.
"Let me work on it.
I'll put my flowers over here."

"Then my yellow sun has to go
down here," said Sheep.

"No, no," said Fox.
"My star goes up here."

"That thing is no star," said Bear.

"Oh!" cried Fox.
He jumped at Bear.
Bear fell over into Donkey.
Donkey fell on Sheep.
Then Sheep, Donkey, Bear,
and Fox all went down.
So did the work of art!
Crack!
It was all over the grass.

"Look what you did!"
screamed Bear.

"Quick, fix it!" cried Fox.

"Too late now," said Sheep.

Wolf and Cat came to find the best work of art.

They looked at the things on the grass.

Wolf looked down and up.
Cat looked up and down.

Then Wolf said, "I like it. I like it a lot."

"I like it, too," said Cat.
"It is just the thing for this park."

"Who made this art?" asked Wolf.

"We all did!" said Bear.

"Then you will all get the prize," said Wolf.

Cat gave the prize to them.
Fox looked at it.
"Read it, Fox," said Donkey.

Fox said, "First prize.
Best art in the show."

"And I said we were not good at art!" said Sheep.

Maria Martinez, Artist

Maria Martinez lives in the West.
She is an artist.
She has worked with clay.
She has made beautiful black pots
out of clay.

Maria's mother had made clay pots.
They were good pots.
But they were not as beautiful
as the black pots Maria made.

Maria made the pots at home.
She worked on the clay.
She made a rope out of it.

Then she bent the rope.
She bent it around and up.
Little by little she made a clay pot.

Mr. Martinez helped her.

He painted pictures on the
sides of the pots.

Then he made a fire.

Maria put the pots in the fire.

Soon the pots were dry.

The pots were black.
They had black paintings on them.
People said that they were the
most beautiful pots of all.

Mobiles

A mobile is art that moves.
This mobile is never still.
Day and night it moves in the air.

You can make a mobile.

You will need the things you see here.

Get some string, and something to cut the string.

Then find things to hang from the string.

A Flower Mobile

To make this mobile, you will
need many flowers.

Find pictures of flowers in old books.
Cut them out.

Paint flowers, too.

Paint them red, and pink, and yellow.

Then make the flower mobile and
hang it up.

It will make you think of summer.

A Junk Mobile

You can make a junk mobile.

Make it from bright things, as you see here.

Make it from old things you have around your house.

Make it from things you find.

Ask your friends to help.

You can have fun making a junk mobile.

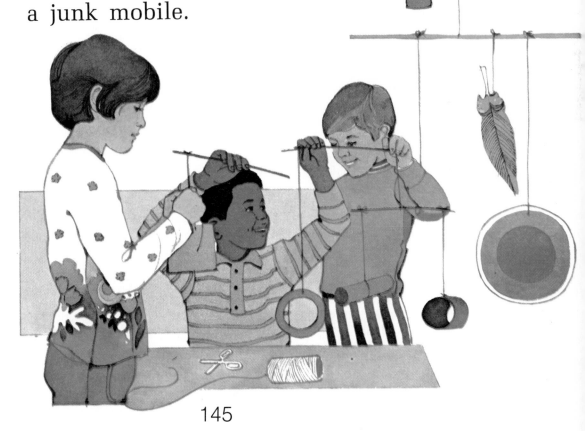

A Sky Mobile

Cut out things for a sky mobile.
Cut out big stars and small stars.
Cut out a big yellow sun.
Make some birds, too.

Here is one girl's mobile.
She likes to see the things move
in the air.

A Bell Mobile

Make a bell mobile with spoons.
Get some big spoons.
Get some small ones, too.
Put strings on the spoons.
Hang the spoons on the mobile.
Then put the mobile outside.
The mobile will move around
and around in the air.
Listen.
Listen to the bells!

The Man Who Painted Birds

Once a man named John Audubon
lived in America.

His father wanted John to work
on the land.

But John did not want to do that.
That was not his plan.

John Audubon wanted to paint.
He walked in the woods.
He sat under the trees.
He looked at birds and animals.
John said, "One day I will paint
pictures of the things I see."

That is what he did.

He left the towns.

He went west, far into the woods of America.

He saw beautiful birds.

He made pictures of them.

John Audubon's first book was
called <u>Birds of America</u>.

It was filled with pictures of birds.

Some people think that they are
the best bird pictures of all time.

Some of the birds that Audubon painted are not in America today.

People hunted for them until not one bird was left.

But we know what the birds looked like.

We know when we look at the beautiful pictures by John Audubon.

(To be read by the teacher.)

For a Bird

I found him lying near the tree;
I folded up his wings.
   Oh, little bird,
   You never heard
   The song that summer sings.

I wrapped him in a shirt I wore
in winter; it was blue.
   Oh, little bird,
   You never heard
   The song I sang to you.

MYRA COHN LIVINGSTON

Bear, the Artist

Bear Paints

Why is the paint all over Bear?

Bear's Pot

Bear made a clay pot.

He left the pot on a chair to dry.

Then Bear went and got a book.

Bear did not remember where he had put the pot.

He sat down to read.

Bear got up and saw that his clay pot had cracked.

Why did the clay pot crack?

159

The Paints

One day Bear made some paintings.
Then he went away.
He did not clean up.
He did not put the tops
back on the paints.

The next day Bear came back.
He wanted to make a new painting.
But he did not do that, for the
paints were too dry.

Why did the paints dry out?

TRY THIS

What can Bear do to clean up the paint?
What can Bear do to fix the pot?
What will water do to paint that
is too dry?

160

I Have a Home

The Bremen Band

For this play you will need children to play

The Dog

Four Robbers

People

The Rooster

The Cat

The Donkey

162

PEOPLE: A woman had a donkey.
The woman said the donkey was
too old to work.
So she sent the donkey away.
The donkey was very sad.

DONKEY: I am not too old to work.
But now I have no home.
And I am so hungry!
What will I do?
I know!
I'll go to Bremen and work in
the band.

PEOPLE: The donkey was happy.
Soon he met a dog.

DOG: I am so hungry!
The man I stayed with said I was
too old, so he sent me away.

DONKEY: It was just like that with me.
But I know what to do.
I am going to Bremen to work
in the band.
Do you want to come with me?

DOG: Yes, I'll go with you.

PEOPLE: The donkey and the dog
went out of the town.
Soon they met a cat.

CAT: I'll tell you something sad.
The man I lived with sent me away.
He said I was too old.

DOG: It was like that with us.

DONKEY: We are going to Bremen
to play in the band.
Will you come with us?

CAT: Yes, I will.

PEOPLE: The friends went by a house.
They saw a rooster.

CAT: What are you running
from, Rooster?

ROOSTER: People are hunting for me.
They say I am too old to work.
They are going to eat me!

DOG: You must get away from here.

DONKEY: Come with us.
We are going to Bremen to play
in the band.

ROOSTER: I will!

PEOPLE: The friends walked and
walked all day.
Night came and they walked
some more.

ROOSTER: It is dark out.
It is time to find a house to stay
in for the night.

CAT: I see a house by that fence.

DOG: If good people live in it, they
will give us something to eat.

DONKEY: Stay here.
I'll go look in the window.

PEOPLE: The donkey went up to
the house.

CAT: What do you see?

DONKEY: I see a room.
I see good things to eat and drink.
I see people with masks on.

CAT: They must be robbers!

DOG: Robbers!
Come, we must think of something.

CAT: What can we do to get them
out of the house?

ROOSTER: I have a plan.

PEOPLE: The rooster told his plan.
The friends did what the
rooster said.
The dog jumped up on the donkey.
The cat jumped up on the dog.
The rooster jumped up on the cat.

CAT: Now we will make the
robbers run away.

ROOSTER: Go!
Cock-a-doodle-doo.

DONKEY: Hee-haw, hee-haw.

DOG: Bow-wow, bow-wow.

CAT: Meow, meow, meow.

ROBBER ONE: What is that?

ROBBER TWO: Help, help, something
is after us!

ROBBER THREE: What can it be?

ROBBER FOUR: Run, run, we have to
get out of here!

PEOPLE: The robbers jumped up
and ran out of the house.
They ran to the hills far away.

DONKEY: The robbers will not come back.
We can go into this beautiful house.

DOG: We can get something to eat.

CAT: We can live here from now on.

ROOSTER: And we do not have to go
to Bremen!

PEOPLE: So the good friends did not
go to Bremen after all.

171

Oh, I Have a Home

Oh, the owl has a home,
Has a home,
Has a home,
Oh, the owl has a home
In the tree.
And so does the fly,
So does the bluebird,
So does the buzzing bee.

Oh, the bear has a home,
Has a home,
Has a home,
Oh, the bear has a home
In the zoo.
And so does the wolf,
So does the fox,
So does the turtle, too.

173

Oh, I have a home,
Have a home,
Have a home,
Oh, I have a home
In a house.
And so does my mother,
So does my father,
So does my little mouse!

174

The Little Gray House

By Lilian Moore

Once a little house was on a hill.

It was an old house.

It was very old and very gray.

It had gray doors and gray windows.

It had gray walls and a gray fence.

A man and a woman lived in the house.

The man and woman did not go out much.

But one beautiful day, they went to see some friends.

They got into their car.
They went uphill and downhill and then uphill and downhill again.
At last they saw the house of their friends.

It was a little red house with white doors and windows.

All around it flowers and green things were growing.

The man and woman had a good time with their friends.

Then they got into their car and went home.

They went uphill and downhill, then uphill and downhill again.

At last they came to their little gray house.

"My," said the woman.

"This house is very gray."

The man said, "It has no grass and flowers outside."

"We must sell this house," said the woman.
"Then we can get a good house."

"One with grass and flowers growing around it," said the man.
So the man and woman tried to sell the house.

First a man came to look.

"No," he said.

"This house is too gray for me.
I like a red house."

He went away.

"Oh, my," said the woman.

"We will paint the house red,"
said the man.

"Then the next one will take it."

So the man and woman painted
the house red.

Soon after, a woman came to look.
"I like a house that has white
windows and doors," she said.
And she went away.

So the man and woman painted
the windows white.
Then they painted the doors and
fence white, too.

Soon after that, a man and
woman came to see the house.

They liked the outside.

"But it is so gray inside," said
the man.

They went away.

So this time the man and woman
painted the inside of the house.

They painted some walls yellow
and some walls blue.

Soon a man came to see the house.

"This is a beautiful house," he said.

"But I am looking for a house with flowers and grass."

And he, too, went away.

The man and woman went to work planting grass and flowers.

Soon green grass was growing.

Then one day flowers came up, red and pink and yellow, all around the house.

"Now," said the woman.
"Someone will want the house now.
Then at last we can get the
house we want."

The man looked around.
Slowly he said, "Tell me about
the house we want."

"Well," said the woman.
"We want a beautiful house."

The man said, "A house that is
painted inside and out?"

"Oh, yes," said the woman.

"With grass and flowers growing
around it?" asked the man.

"Oh, yes!" said the woman.

The man laughed.
"Look around you!" he said.

So the woman looked around.

She saw a red house with white
windows and doors and a white fence.

Inside she saw bright yellow
and blue walls.

Outside she saw grass and flowers.

"Well!" said the woman in surprise. "This is a beautiful house."

"This is just the house we want," said the man.

So the man and woman lived in
the little gray house on the hill.
But now it was not a little gray
house at all.

New Words

school
crosses
stop
train
lot
rock
boat

time
rain
wasn't
didn't
of
top
teacher
odd

Ben
show
pet
ask

well
live
children

frog
air
egg
tadpole
under
leg
front

wheat
four
myself
end
flour
bake
sent
best

set
first

paint
picture
side
inside
outside

woman
clay
climb
crack
glad
cried

great
break
scream
more
door
tree

made
race
mad

walk
take
wake
late
now

name
line
book
five
paper
once
read

wood
those
log
drive
rope
mill
soft

nest
wasp

does
spot
chew
room
small

sheet
zoo
has
next

other
circus
yellow
color
be
gentle

sing
want
feather
bird
grand
hide

luck
rid

Luis Martinez
shoes
Chet
their
remember
white
window

Betsy
tomorrow
old
spent
stand
told
stay

skip
move
scold
wish

Unit openers, pages 5, 33, 65, 97, 129, 161: Oni
Melanie Arwin: 172-174; David Brown: 98; Marc Brown: 20-24; Victoria Chess: 30; Peter Cross: 13, Renée Daily: 79-82; Diane Dawson: 105-110; Diane de Groat: 158; Michael Eagle: 75; Len Ebert: 116-126, 143-147; Creston Ely: 83-86; Frank Fretz: 25-29; Jürg Furrer: 55-59; Michael Garland: 148, 150, 152, 154, 156; Michael Hampshire: 6-12, 138-140; Richard Hefter: 130-136; Robert Jackson: 41-44; Lionel Kalish: 45-54; Al Lorenz: 70-74; Sal Murdocca: 34-40; Jan Palmer: 99-104; Diane Paterson: 14-19; Jan Pyk: 60-62; Don Silverstein: 162-171; Maggie Swanson: 175-189; Joseph Veno: 87-94.

All photographs are HARBRACE except those listed below: KEY: l, (left); r, (right)

Page 66, Gene Ahrens/Shostal; 69(l), Bettmann Archive; 69(r), Field Museum of Natural History; 76, Hans Pfletschinger/Peter Arnold; 77, C.Z. Momatiuk/Photo Researchers; 78, Hans Pfletschinger/Peter Arnold; 111, Victoria Beller-Smith; 112, Marion Faller/Monkmeyer; 113, Terri Bisbee; 114, Victoria Beller-Smith; 115, George Ancona; 137, 141, Susan Peterson; 142, Museum of Modern Art; 149, 151, 153, 155, 157, New York Historical Society.

A
B
C
D
E
F
G
H
I
J